Under the Lights

Under the Lights
A Child Model at Work

by
Barbara Beirne

 Carolrhoda Books, Inc. • Minneapolis

The author would like to thank Michelle, her family, and her friends, whose warmth and enthusiasm made this project fun and full of surprises. Jade Albert, Bert Rockfield, and their staffs deserve special thanks for inviting me into their busy lives. I'm also indebted to Monica Stewart of Schuller Talent, who helped me find the perfect model. The author would also like to thank Bloomingdale's for the courtesy that they extended to her in allowing her to photograph their back-to-school fashion show.

The photograph on pages 20 and 21 is reproduced through the courtesy of Michael Ian.
The photograph on page 46 is reproduced through the courtesy of Jade Albert.

Copyright © 1988 by Carolrhoda Books

LIBRARY OF CONGRESS CATALOGING-IN-PUBLICATION DATA

Beirne, Barbara.
    Under the lights : a child model at work / Barbara Beirne.
        p.   cm.
        Summary: Eleven-year-old Michelle describes how she became a fashion model and her career in ads, commercials, and fashion shows.
        ISBN 0-87614-316-8 (lib. bdg.)
        1. Models, Fashion—United States—Juvenile literature.
    [1. Models, Fashion. 2. Occupations.] I. Title.
    HD6073.M772U53 1988
    659.1'52—dc19   88-440
                                                       CIP
                                                       AC

Manufactured in the United States of America

1 2 3 4 5 6 7 8 9 10 98 97 96 95 94 93 92 91 90 89 88

For John

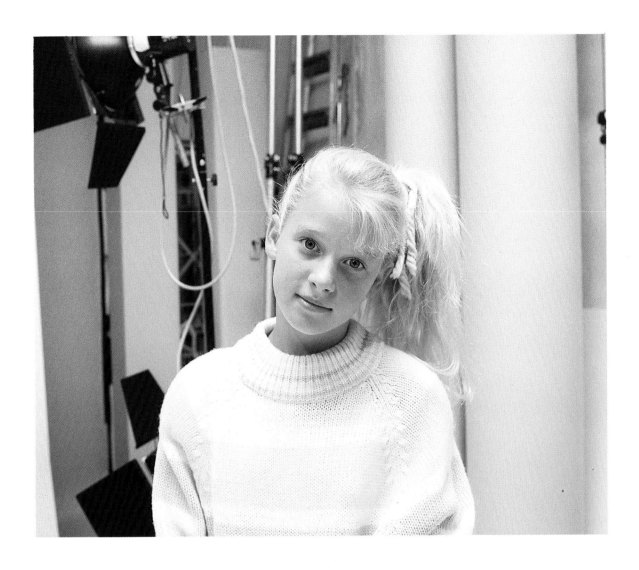

My name is Michelle Bush, and I'm 11 years old. I'm a professional model.

When I was 5 years old, my mother took me to see a musical show. I thought it would be fun to be onstage. I joined a children's theater group called the Make Believe Players. When they presented the musical *Annie*, I played the part of Mollie, the youngest orphan. I was sure I would be nervous, but I wasn't. Mollie is a funny little girl, and as soon as the audience laughed, I felt happy and started having a good time onstage.

I acted with amateur groups and in school productions. When I was in third grade, something happened that changed my life. Tanner Mullen, a professional model, and I were in a school play together. Tanner told me that modeling is a form of acting, since you have to perform in front of a camera. A photographer might ask you to be happy, or sad, or serious. You have to be able to concentrate and change your expression quickly.

Tanner said, "Why don't you try modeling?"

Me—a model! I thought it was a great idea, but it took a long time to convince my parents.

We live in Pennsylvania, but most of the modeling jobs in this area for children are in New York City. That meant someone would have to go with me to New York, then stay and chaperon while I was on modeling assignments.

My mother thought modeling would be an interesting experience for both of us. Luckily, my brother and sister are grown up, and Mom has the time to travel back and forth from Pennsylvania to New York.

There was still one problem, though. My parents were afraid I would miss too much school. I decided right then to work extra hard in school. Each time I brought home my report card, I reminded Mom and Dad that my dream was to be a model.

Finally, Mom and Dad agreed to write a letter to a model agency to get information about being a model. Dad took a snapshot of me, and we sent it in with the letter.

Waiting for an answer was hard. I talked to my cockatiel, whose name is Ramy. "Do you think I will be lucky enough to model?" I would ask him.

Sometimes I played catch with our dog, Maggie. Her real name is Lady Margaret of Furlong, but we never call her that. Maggie is an Airedale terrier.

My friends Meredith, Ashley, and Carrie and I practiced being models in my backyard.

We even put on makeup and pretended we were getting ready for a big shoot. Photography sessions are often called shoots by the professionals.

Practicing with my friends was fun, but I was beginning to think I would always be just a pretend model.

Then one day, Monica Stewart phoned from the model agency and asked me to come in for an interview. Mom and I went to Monica's office in New York City. I was really nervous, but Mom tried to calm me down. She said, "Just look at this as an interesting experience."

Finally, my name was called, and I went in alone to meet Monica. She asked me lots of questions about why I wanted to be a model. She explained that only a few child models are successful and modeling takes a considerable amount of hard work.

Next, I had to read a short commercial. When I finished, Monica said, "When do you want to start?"

I couldn't believe it. I was really going to be a model!

Back in Pennsylvania, my mom and I went to see the principal of my school, Dr. Robert Barth. I crossed my fingers when Mom asked, "Would it be all right for Michelle to miss school occasionally in order to pursue a career in modeling?" Dr. Barth said that since I was a good student, he would approve. But he warned me that if my grades started to drop, I would have to decide between a career and an education.

I also had a long talk with my dad. He explained that modeling is not a game but a serious business. All the people involved are earning a living. They would be depending on me to act responsibly. I would be well paid, but I would have to make sacrifices without complaining. Dad said I would have to give up my after-school activities, and I would probably miss birthday parties and other fun things with my friends.

I wanted to go on doing things with my friends— but I wanted to be a model, too. I promised Dad I would work hard and wouldn't complain.

Michelle
Bush

Getting ready to be a model cost some money. The model agency sent me to a photographer. Then the agency selected two of the photos he took to be used for my composite, or head sheet. This is a sheet given out to clients that has my picture, my measurements, and my date of birth on it. We had to pay a photog-

SIZE_____HT_____SHOE_____
HAIR_____EYES_____BORN_____
AGE RANGE_____

rapher and then a printer for 150 black-and-white
composite sheets.

We had to buy four pairs of shoes that would be
used only for modeling. Photographers don't like their
models to wear dirty sneakers!

I also went to the doctor for a checkup. That's required before you can get a Child Model Permit from the city of New York. There is no charge for the permit, but it has to be renewed each year.

Hooray! I was finally ready to start modeling. My mom and I began going to New York to attend go-sees. A go-see is just what it sounds like. Your agent sends you to see someone, usually a photographer or an advertising director. This person decides if you are the right model for the job.

Sometimes when you arrive at a studio, you are seen right away. Other times, you have to wait in a long line. This kind of go-see is jokingly called a cattle call. It isn't much fun.

Often on go-sees, you try on the actual clothes the photographer will be using for the shoot. When I went to Jade Albert's studio on a go-see, she took a Polaroid photo of me in a baseball shirt. The picture was marked with my name, my height, and my dress size.

After everyone has been seen, the kids selected are notified by their model agency. The agency usually calls them late in the afternoon to schedule their modeling jobs for the next day. It is important to be available. If models turn down too many jobs, they'll stop getting called.

I went on a lot of go-sees. The photographers were very nice, but they always seemed to choose an experienced model instead of me. Sometimes the clothes didn't fit me, or the photographer would say, "Sorry, we need a brunette."

My mom and I became experts at finding our way around New York City. After long, busy days, she would often ask me, "Michelle, are you sure you want to do this?"

I always said yes.

Just when I was starting to get discouraged, I got my first booking! A modeling assignment is called a booking. I would be working for Bert Rockfield. Bert is a well-known photographer who specializes in taking pictures for newspapers and magazines.

Mom and I were supposed to be in New York by eight o'clock in the morning, so we had to leave our house while it was still dark. On the way, I slept in the back seat of the car.

When we arrived at the studio, the first person I met was Barbara Ferry, who is Bert Rockfield's stylist. She said that the best definition of her job is "chief cook and bottle washer" because she does a little of everything.

Usually, child models wear very little makeup. Barbara likes to use a bit of cover-up under the eyes, and some blush and lip gloss. Sometimes she puts light eye shadow on the girls.

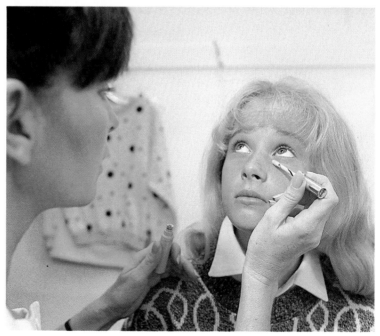

Hinda Rubinstein, the studio seamstress, made sure
that the clothes I was going to wear looked just right.
She would iron them or even alter them if necessary.

After I put on my first outfit, Barbara selected some jewelry to go with my sweater. The studio has a huge closet filled with all kinds of accessories. Wouldn't it be great to have something like that at home!

The set in a photography studio is like a stage. There are huge lights on stands and hanging from the ceiling. Umbrellas are set up to reflect and soften the light, which makes it more flattering to the model. Big fans are turned on to make it look as if the model's hair is blowing in the wind.

Bert's assistant, Michael Bonacci, used a light meter to measure the light. This is how photographers determine the exposure for the film.

Bert was very patient. He knew it was my first booking, and he carefully gave me instructions on what to do. He asked me to hold a fishing pole and stand on the seamless paper. My job was to concentrate and to follow all his directions. I was surprised that I felt so comfortable in front of the camera. I wasn't nervous at all.

Although it takes a long time to set up the proper lighting, the actual photographing goes very quickly. Bert usually takes 40 pictures of each outfit in about 15 minutes.

Now I'm a real model!

When the photography session was over, Mom and I celebrated my first job by going shopping.

My parents and I agreed that the money I earned from modeling would be put into a savings account for my college education. But this day, Mom let me buy a new backpack for school.

As the weeks go by, my agent calls more frequently with go-sees and bookings. It takes a lot of planning to work out a schedule so there is time for both school and modeling. Sometimes I go to school early to look at filmstrips. After classes in the morning, my teacher gives me the afternoon assignments. Then I leave to go to my modeling job.

Mom and I discover that the best way to get to New York City is to drive to Trenton, New Jersey, and take the train from there. On the way to the train station, I study in the car. Then, while Mom parks the car, I rush to the train and save two seats. Jim is my favorite train conductor. He loves to tell jokes, and he even thinks some of my jokes are funny.

If there is going to be a big test in school, I call the model agency and book-out, or tell them I won't be available. Then they know not to schedule any jobs for me that day.

The more modeling jobs I do, the more professional my portfolio looks. A portfolio is a kind of scrapbook with a handle. In it, I keep samples of the modeling work I've done for magazines, newspapers, and catalogs. Art directors look through portfolios at go-sees.

Working on location is the most fun. The term "on location" means taking photographs somewhere other than a studio. Today I am booked all day to model for Jade Albert, a children's fashion photographer. The pictures she takes will be in a back-to-school catalog.

When we are on location, a house trailer serves as
a temporary studio. In it is a makeup table and room
for the models to change clothes. The clothes are stored
in the trailer. The little bit of space that is left can
be used for resting between shots.

Jade uses a 35-mm camera that is mounted on a
tripod, or three-legged stand. She is almost 40 feet
away from the models because she wants pictures with
a short depth of field. This means that in the final
photographs, the models can be seen clearly, but the
background will look blurry. Jade uses a slide film
called Ektachrome. The film is kept in an ice chest
because if it gets hot, there can be slight changes in
the colors of the photographs.

For the first shot of the day, the lighting director
sets up a scrim over our heads to filter the sunlight.
A scrim is a white nylon cloth anchored to a heavy
stand. Without it, the sun would create dark shadows
on our faces.

After lunch we have time to put on our own clothes and play in the park. One of the things I like most about modeling is all the new friends I've made. Amber, Taina, and I talk about school and modeling. My favorite model is Brooke Shields.

Amber goes to a special school in New York City for children who work. Most of the students are actors, musicians, or models.

The lighting is very complicated for the final shot of the day. We wait on the set a long time for everything to be ready. It's hard to have to sit that long. When some kids from the neighborhood come over to talk to us, we explain that we're working and have to pay attention to the photographer and her staff.

This is one of Jade Albert's photographs from our day on location. Doesn't Tara's hair look cute? The hair-stylist wires her pigtails so they curl up in a funny way.

Although I love days on location, they aren't easy. When the photography session ends at six o'clock, Mom and I have a two-hour trip home. When we get back to Pennsylvania, I have to eat dinner. Then I still have some homework to finish. It takes me longer to do my homework now than before I started modeling because I miss some of the teacher's explanations.

Each modeling assignment is different. I never know
what will be next. Fashion shows are always interesting
to do. Sometimes there are rehearsals, other times
there aren't. I always have to act like I love what
I'm wearing. This is when my acting experience helps
me the most.

During a fashion show, I walk up and down the runway while an announcer describes the clothes I'm modeling. The audience smiles and applauds. After working in a studio, it's fun to get some audience reaction. I can always tell what outfits they like the best.

Mom and I have some wonderful days in New York City. When I roller-skate to some of my assignments, Mom has a hard time keeping up with me. Wow! There's someone who looks familiar. It really feels funny to see a picture of myself.

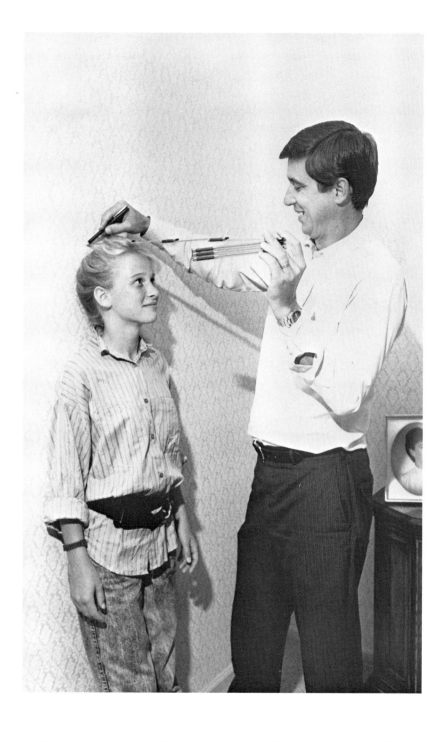

For over a year, I've been modeling about four days a week. Then something happens. I start getting fewer bookings. The clothes I try on at go-sees are often too small. Dad measures me at home, and we find that I've grown 6 inches in 12 months.

I'm getting too big to be a child model. Mom and
Dad think that since I'm starting junior high, this
would be a good time for me to retire from modeling.
Mom says that even if I stop modeling, I can still visit
New York and see my friends Taina and Amber.

It's a hard decision to make.

After thinking it over, though, I decide to stop modeling. Maybe I'll model again when I grow up because even with the hard work it has been a lot of fun. I've met all kinds of interesting people, made many new friends, and saved some money for college.

Modeling was a dream I had that came true. Maybe
now it's time to work on something else for a while.
I have lots of dreams, but they can wait. After all,
I'm only 11 years old.

ABOUT THE AUTHOR

Barbara Beirne is a graduate of Marymount College and recently received her M.F.A. from Pratt Institute. She has been a professional free-lance photographer for 12 years and her work has been exhibited in galleries in New York and New Jersey. As a photojournalist, her work has appeared in magazines and newspapers. Ms. Beirne lives in Morris Township in New Jersey with her husband, a doctor. They have four children and one grandchild. This is her second book for children.